bake me I'm yours...

Cupcake Fun

Carolyn White

D&C
David and Charles

contents

have some cupcake fun!

When I started my cake-making company 10 years ago, every order was all about having fun with different sizes of cake and icing in order to make the celebration in question memorable. Over the following years, customers have continued to challenge my team in their desire to see their varied hobbies and interests re-created in sugar and popped on top of a cake or cupcake. So this book brings lots of those simple, interesting ideas together to create delicious cupcakes for every occasion that really will make both kids and adults smile. These little cakes make great party centrepieces or gifts to show how much you care, or simply an entertaining family treat. The cake bases and frostings can be mixed and matched and used for any project you choose to decorate them with, or eat them just as they are for an everyday bite.

This book has been devised for those new to making cupcakes as well as those who are looking to expand their skills, whether with new flavours, designs or decorating techniques, and as a helpful guide each project has a skill rating indicated by one, two or three cupcake symbols.

I hope you enjoy learning some new recipes to bake and experimenting with tasty toppings to create, and don't forget to sample them along the way – cook's perks!

Have fun!

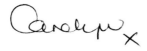

tools & equipment

Before you start, it's a good idea to check you have everything to hand that you might need. Included in this section is a list of essential equipment for making and baking your cupcake sponge bases and to whip up your frostings; a basic decorating toolbox; and key specialist tools. Don't feel you need to have all the latter kit to create fun cupcakes, but if you are making a large quantity or get really hooked, these are the items I find really useful. Specific tools required beyond the basics are listed under 'you will need' at the start of each project.

baking essentials

☆ Kitchen scales/measuring cups and measuring spoons – for accurately weighing ingredients

☆ Electric stand mixer with paddle attachment (flat beater) – to make the sponge cake bases and toppings

☆ Muffin and mini muffin trays (pans)

☆ Wire rack – to cool cupcakes

☆ Flexible plastic spatulas – for scraping out bowls

☆ Muffin baking cases (liners) – keep a variety of the many fantastic designs available, both paper and foil, on hand for spontaneous events

☆ Large disposable plastic piping (pastry) bags – for piping your mixture into cases (liners)

☆ Oven thermometer – a must if unsure of your internal oven temperature

☆ Microwave or double boiler – for melting chocolate

☆ Plastic or glass microwave-safe bowls – for melting chocolate and butter

☆ Sieve (strainer)

We usually use muffin or mini muffin-size baking cases (liners) because they are just the right size to be flat-frosted to present your cupcakes beautifully and still give a perfect amount of sponge. Smaller cupcake or fairy cake cases are not suitable for these projects.

basic decorating toolbox

☆ Non-stick work board with non-stick mat beneath to prevent slipping – to roll out icing and cut out and model paste shapes

☆ Non-stick rolling pin – for rolling out sugarpaste (rolled fondant) and flower (petal/gum) paste

☆ Icing spacers – to achieve an even 3mm (⅛in) thickness

☆ Large disposable plastic piping (pastry) bags, 46cm (18in) or 53cm (21in) – for piping frostings

☆ Paper piping (pastry) bags – made from baking (parchment) paper for small quantities of royal icing/applying details

☆ Piping tubes (tips) – fine for piping royal icing details; large for piping frosting (see Techniques: Applying Frostings)

☆ Scissors – to snip the ends of piping (pastry) bags for tubes (tips) to fit snugly

☆ Large and mini palette knives – large for buttercream; mini for cutting, turning paste and lifting paste shapes/features

☆ Paintbrushes – a selection of sable (no. 3 for glue) and pony (no. 8 for glitter) are handy

☆ Set of 11 circle cutters (Ateco) – nos. specified count outwards from the smallest, no. 1

☆ Icing smoother – for smoothing and polishing sugarpaste (rolled fondant)

☆ Sugar glue – for attaching decorative elements

☆ Cocktail sticks (toothpicks) – for applying colour to icing and creating tiny indentations

specialist decorating items

☆ Shaped cutters – ovals, hearts, square, star, triangle

☆ Kemper mini plunger cutters – 4mm (⅛in) circle and heart are used in many projects; PME blossom set comes with a foam pad to push the plunger against to cup the paste

☆ Ball tool and smile tool (PME) – for adding detail to paste characters

☆ Dresden tool – for scoring lines into paste and adding texture

☆ Paint palette – for mixing colours and blending gold/silver lustre dust with alcohol

☆ Dusting brush – for brushing lustre dust onto paste

☆ Foiled cake board – for storing made-ahead paste discs

recipes

Now that you have all your basic equipment to hand, you are ready to begin your preparations for baking. You can use almost any recipe for the decorated cupcake projects in this book, and I have listed some of my special favourites here for you to choose from.

cupcake recipes

First, get to know the Golden Rules of Baking before you proceed. I always use a stand mixer and where possible give easy 'all-in-one' recipes, but if you wish to make your cake mix by hand, cream the fat and sugar together in a mixing bowl with a wooden spoon until light and fluffy before gradually beating in any liquids and finally incorporating the flour with a large metal spoon.

golden rules of baking

☆ Let all your ingredients come to room temperature before you begin to make your cake mix.

☆ Before starting to make your cupcakes, read the recipe right through to familiarize yourself with the method.

☆ Preheat your oven and check that it is reaching the correct temperature by using an oven thermometer.

☆ Prepare tins (pans) before starting to make your cake mix so that it doesn't have to sit.

☆ Ensure you weigh the ingredients accurately – the key to great cupcakes!

☆ Never cream your mixture on full speed – start on slow and work upwards.

☆ Eggs are best used when they are at room temperature.

☆ Add eggs one at a time or gradually to prevent curdling, adding a tablespoon of the flour if it looks like the mixture may be starting to curdle.

☆ Always fold in the flour. If using a mixer, use the paddle attachment (flat beater) on the slowest speed.

☆ Generally fill the muffin baking cases (liners) two-thirds full for a flat top and to allow room for frosting.

☆ If your oven has a hot spot, rotate the pan halfway through baking.

☆ Use a wire rack to help your cakes cool quickly.

cupcake troubleshooting

Peaked – either too much raising agent or the oven temperature is too hot

Sunken – not cooked for long enough or oven door opened too soon

Sloping – check with a spirit level that your oven shelves or even the oven itself is level

Some cooked but others not quite – your oven may have a hot spot, so the muffin tray (pan) needs to be rotated halfway through the cupcake baking time

Dense or heavy texture – mixture not thoroughly mixed together and the raising agent hasn't been distributed evenly; can also be caused by overbeating the mixture

Any baked but undecorated cupcakes can either be frozen for a treat another day (up to a month in an airtight box) or used to create cake pops – see *Bake Me I'm Yours… Cake Pops* for ideas.

US cup measurements

If you prefer to use cup measurements, please use the following conversions.
(Note: 1 Australian tbsp = 20ml.)

liquid

1 tsp = 5ml
1 tbsp = 15ml
½ cup = 120ml/4fl oz
1 cup = 240ml/8½fl oz

butter

1 tbsp = 15g/½oz
2 tbsp = 25g//1oz
½ cup/1 stick = 115g/4oz
1 cup/2 sticks = 225g/8oz

caster (superfine) sugar/brown sugar

½ cup = 100g/3½oz
1 cup = 200g/7oz

icing (confectioners') sugar

1 cup = 115g/4oz

flour

1 cup = 125g/4½oz

ground almonds

½ cup = 50g/1¾oz

chopped nuts

1 cup = about 125g (4¼oz)

cream cheese

1 cup = 225g (8oz)

classic vanilla

Light and luscious, this vanilla sponge recipe will never fail to produce a great sponge base for the most fabulous decorations. If you fancy a change for a more zingy flavour, simply follow the suggestions for a citrus version.

you will need...
makes about 12

☆ 125g (4½oz) margarine, softened

☆ 125g (4½oz) caster (superfine) sugar

☆ 1 tsp (5ml) vanilla extract

☆ 2 eggs (medium or large), lightly beaten

☆ 125g (4½oz) self-raising (-rising) flour

☆ 2 tbsp (30ml) milk

1 Preheat the oven to 200°C/fan 180°C/400°F/Gas Mark 6. Line your muffin tray (pan) with muffin cases (liners) and set to one side.

2 Place the margarine, sugar and vanilla extract in the bowl of an electric stand mixer and cream together until light and fluffy.

3 Add the eggs gradually and then sift the flour into the mixture and combine on a low speed. Add the milk to make a smooth dropping consistency.

4 Spoon the mixture evenly into the cases or fill a large disposable plastic piping (pastry) bag with the batter, snip off the end and pipe it into the muffin cases.

5 Bake for 25–28 minutes, or until risen and springy to the touch. Cool on a wire rack.

To vary the flavour of the sponge, for lemon or orange, replace the vanilla extract with a teaspoon of lemon or orange oil. For a more zingy citrus taste, add the finely grated zest of one washed unwaxed lemon or orange. For a chocolate chip option, add 100g (3½oz) dark (semisweet or bittersweet) or milk chocolate chips.

double chocolate

If you want a really good, dependable chocolate cupcake recipe, this is the one. The cakes keep well and are great for decorating, but they are also ideal just with a cream cheese frosting or a decadent chocolate frosting.

you will need...
makes about 12

☆ 112g (4oz) butter, cut into pieces

☆ 75g (2¾oz) dark (semisweet or bittersweet) chocolate callets or pieces

☆ 150g (5½oz) caster (superfine) sugar

☆ 60g (2¼oz) self-raising (-rising) flour

☆ 1½ tbsp cocoa powder (unsweetened cocoa)

☆ ½ tsp baking powder

☆ 3 large eggs, beaten

1 Preheat the oven to 190°C/fan 170°C/375°F/Gas Mark 5. Line your muffin tray (pan) with muffin cases (liners) and set to one side.

2 Put the butter and chocolate in a microwave-safe bowl and place in a microwave oven on low for about 2 minutes, checking often, until melted. Stir in the sugar and then leave to cool.

3 Meanwhile, sift the flour, cocoa and baking powder together into the bowl of an electric stand mixer bowl.

4 Add the eggs along with the melted chocolate mixture to the dry ingredients. Beat on the slowest setting and then increase the speed gradually for 2–3 minutes, or until well combined.

5 Using a spatula, fill a large disposable plastic piping (pastry) bag with the batter, sniff off the end and pipe into the cases, or spoon the mixture evenly into the cases.

6 Bake for 20–25 minutes, or until risen and springy to the touch. Cool on a wire rack.

blueberry & almond

Children and adults alike will love these fresh and fruity cupcakes, and they'll also provide you with one of your five-a-day fruits! You can try using other berries in place of the blueberries, such as luscious raspberries.

you will need...

makes about 12

- ☆ 175g (6oz) unsalted butter, softened
- ☆ 175g (6oz) caster (superfine) sugar
- ☆ 175g (6oz) self-raising (-rising) flour
- ☆ 1 tsp baking powder
- ☆ 3 large eggs, beaten
- ☆ 3 tbsp ground almonds
- ☆ 150g (5½oz) blueberries

1 Preheat the oven to 180°C/fan 160°C/350°F/ Gas Mark 4. Line your muffin tray (pan) with muffin cases (liners) and set to one side.

2 Place the butter, sugar, flour, baking powder and eggs in the bowl of an electric stand mixer. Beat on a slow speed and then increase the speed gradually for 2–3 minutes, or until well combined.

3 Stir in the ground almonds and blueberries.

4 Spoon the mixture evenly into the cases.

5 Bake for 18 minutes, or until risen and golden brown. Cool on a wire rack.

strawberry jam surprise

These delicious cupcakes have ground almonds added to the mixture for extra flavour. But the real wow factor here is the lovely jammy surprise you experience when you bite into the sponge. You will need a long, narrow piping tube for piping the jam into the baked cake centres.

you will need...
makes about 12

☆ 115g (4oz) margarine or salted butter, softened

☆ 115g (4oz) caster (superfine) sugar

☆ 115g (4oz) self-raising (-rising) flour

☆ 55g (2oz) ground almonds

☆ 2 large eggs, beaten

☆ 3 tbsp (45ml) milk

for the filling:

☆ about 4 tbsp strawberry jam

☆ no. 230 (Bismarck) piping tube (tip)

1 Preheat the oven to 180°C/fan 160°C/350°F/Gas Mark 4. Line your muffin tray (pan) with muffin cases (liners) and set to one side.

2 Place all the ingredients in the bowl of an electric stand mixer. Beat on a slow speed and then increase the speed gradually for 2–3 minutes, or until well combined.

3 Spoon the mixture evenly into the cases or fill a large disposable plastic piping (pastry) bag with the batter, snip off the end and pipe it into the cases.

4 Bake for 15–20 minutes, or until risen and golden brown. Cool on a wire rack.

5 When cool, fill another piping bag fitted with the no. 230 piping tube with the jam. Insert downwards into the centre of each cupcake and squeeze about a teaspoonful of jam into the cake centre, withdrawing the tube as you go.

chocolate brownie

This makes fantastic cupcakes, but a word of warning – only choose this recipe if you have made your decorations and frostings in advance, as you need to bake, cool, decorate and eat these cupcakes in one day or they will turn crispy.

you will need...
makes about 12

☆ 225g (8oz) dark (semisweet or bittersweet) chocolate pieces, callets or buttons

☆ 85g (3oz) salted butter, cut into pieces

☆ 2 large eggs, beaten

☆ 200g (7oz) soft dark brown sugar

☆ 140g (5oz) plain (all-purpose) flour

☆ 1 tsp (5ml) vanilla extract

☆ 75g (2¾oz) pecan nuts, chopped

1 Preheat the oven to 180°C/fan 160°C/350°F/ Gas Mark 4. Line your muffin tray (pan) with muffin cases (liners) and set to one side.

2 Put the chocolate and butter in a microwave-safe bowl and place in a microwave oven on low for about 2 minutes, checking often, until melted. Stir well and leave to cool.

3 Meanwhile, place the eggs and sugar in the bowl of an electric stand mixer and beat on a medium speed. Add the vanilla extract and melted chocolate mixture and beat again. Spoon in the flour and mix on a slow speed until combined, then add the pecan nuts and mix again.

4 Spoon the mixture evenly into the cases or fill a large disposable plastic piping (pastry) bag with the batter, snip off the end allowing a large enough hole for the nuts and pipe it into the cases.

5 Bake for 25–30 minutes, or until firm to the touch but you will want them to be slightly moist in the centre. Cool on a wire rack.

banana & macadamia

These cupcakes are tantalizingly exotic tasting, with their tropical fruit, rich nuts and warm spice. You can also use natural (plain) yogurt or sour cream instead of the buttermilk.

you will need...
makes 12–15

☆ 210g (7½oz) plain (all-purpose) flour

☆ 1 tsp bicarbonate of soda (baking soda)

☆ ¼ tsp salt

☆ ½ tsp ground cinnamon

☆ ⅛ tsp allspice

☆ 125g (4½oz) unsalted butter, softened

☆ 300g (10½oz) caster (superfine) sugar

☆ 2 large eggs

☆ ½ tsp (2.5ml) vanilla extract

☆ 100ml (3½fl oz) buttermilk

☆ 1–2 overripe bananas, depending on size, mashed

☆ 60g (2¼oz) macadamia nuts, chopped

1 Preheat the oven to 170°C/fan 140°C/325°F/Gas Mark 3. Line your muffin trays (pans) with muffin cases (liners) and set to one side.

2 Sift the flour, bicarbonate of soda, salt and spices together into a bowl.

3 Place the butter in the bowl of an electric stand mixer and cream for 1–2 minutes. Add the sugar and beat until the mixture is light and fluffy.

4 Add the eggs one at a time, beating for 1 minute after each addition, or until the mixture is light and fluffy. Add the vanilla extract and beat until combined.

5 Add a third of the flour mixture to the creamed mixture and mix on low speed until combined, then add half the buttermilk and banana and mix again. Repeat this process. Add the remaining third of the flour mixture and beat until well combined; don't overbeat, as this will toughen the mixture. Add the nuts and beat again until evenly combined.

6 Spoon the mixture evenly into the cases. Bake for 20 minutes, or until a fine skewer inserted into the centre comes out clean. Cool on a wire rack.

topping recipes

A cupcake is nothing without its finishing touch of decadent frosting, and there are lots of sumptuous recipes to choose from here to suit a variety of tastes.

lemon cream cheese frosting

When using this lovely zingy yet creamy frosting, it's best to frost and decorate only at the last moment because the frosting needs to remain cool (it should always be kept in the fridge), but sugarpaste decorations don't like going in the fridge.

you will need...

☆ 160g (5¾oz) cream cheese

☆ 60g (2¼oz) butter, softened

☆ 2 tsp finely grated lemon zest (unwaxed)

☆ 480g (1lb 1oz) icing (confectioners') sugar, sifted

1 Place the cream cheese, butter and lemon zest in the bowl of an electric stand mixer or mixing bowl and beat until light and fluffy.

2 Gradually beat in the sugar until well combined.

For an orange cream cheese frosting, simply replace the lemon zest with the same quantity of orange zest from a washed unwaxed orange.

whipped chocolate frosting

I love this frosting as a lighter alternative to ganache. It's great for kids, as it is more buttery – plus it's so easy to make. Either spread directly onto your cakes with a palette knife or spoon into a large disposable piping (pastry) bag fitted with a piping tube (tip) and pipe on (see Techniques: Applying Frostings).

you will need...

☆ 200ml (7fl oz) double (heavy) cream

☆ 150g (5½oz) plain (semisweet) chocolate, finely chopped or callets

☆ 280g (10oz) icing (confectioners') sugar, sifted

☆ 140g (5oz) unsalted butter, softened

1 Place the cream in a microwave-safe bowl and heat in a microwave oven until boiling. Add the chocolate and stir until smooth.

2 Leave to cool for 30 minutes, stirring occasionally as it thickens.

3 Place the sugar and butter in a separate bowl and beat until smooth, then beat the cooled chocolate mixture into the butter mixture. Chill for 25 minutes.

Throughout the recipes I mention chocolate 'callets', the term for high-quality Belgium chocolate that I always use in preference to ordinary chocolate bars. It comes in small buttons that melt quickly without burning or splitting and produce the best flavour, so always try to use these if you can.

vanilla buttercream

This is what my kids love more than anything – sweet, fluffy vanilla buttercream just piped in a swirl as the finishing flourish to an irresistible cake! For really generous swirls, use the larger quantities listed.

you will need...

☆ 250g (9oz) lightly salted butter, softened

☆ 500g (1lb 2oz) icing (confectioners') sugar

☆ 2½ tbsp (38ml) water

☆ ½ tsp (2.5ml) vanilla extract

or

☆ 500g (1lb 2oz) lightly salted butter, softened

☆ 1kg (2lb 4oz) icing (confectioners') sugar

☆ 5 tbsp (75ml) water

☆ 1 tsp (5ml) vanilla extract

1 Place the butter in the bowl of an electric stand mixer. Sift over the sugar.
2 Add the water and vanilla extract and beat on slow speed, then increase the speed to high and beat until light and fluffy.

For a lemon buttercream, add a little good-quality lemon oil to taste, and for an orange buttercream, finely grate the zest of a washed unwaxed orange and mix into the buttercream.

chocolate buttercream

This topping never fails to please, but just be sure to use Belgian chocolate callets so that they melt evenly and give you a wonderfully intense flavour.

you will need...

☆ 250g dark (semisweet or bittersweet) chocolate callets

☆ 500g (1lb 2oz) salted butter, softened

☆ 500g (1lb 2oz) icing (confectioners') sugar, sifted

1 Put the chocolate callets in a plastic jug and place in a microwave oven on low for 2 minutes, checking often, until melted.

2 Place the butter and sugar in the bowl of an electric stand mixer and cream on a slow speed. Add the melted chocolate and beat on a high speed until soft and light.

lemon curd buttercream

Fresh, fruity, tangy and sweet – all the taste buds come alive with this tantalizing topping. Try different brands of lemon curd to find the best for you, or why not have a go and make your own? Use the smaller quantity for paletting onto your cupcakes; the larger quantity for piping (see Techniques: Applying Frostings).

you will need...

☆ 65g (2¼oz) salted butter, softened

☆ 100g (3½oz) lemon curd

☆ 125g (4½oz) icing (confectioners') sugar

or

☆ 125g (4½oz) salted butter, softened

☆ 200g (7oz) lemon curd

☆ 250g (9oz) icing (confectioners') sugar

1 Beat the butter until light, then beat in the lemon curd. Sift over the sugar.

2 Continue to beat the buttercream mixture until it is light and fluffy.

dark chocolate ganache

Ganache is the basis of all chocolate truffles, and this recipe turns a simple cupcake into a luxurious treat. This is definitely a topping that the adults will appreciate!

you will need...

☆ 500g (1lb 2oz) double (heavy) cream

☆ 120g (4¼oz) glucose

☆ 500g (1lb 2oz) dark (semisweet or bittersweet) chocolate callets

1 Place the cream and glucose together in a microwave-safe bowl and heat in a microwave oven until boiling.

2 Pour over the chocolate callets in a separate bowl and stir until smooth. Allow to cool. Use the following day.

milk, white or strawberry chocolate ganache

Make these toppings in just the same way as the dark chocolate ganache.

you will need...

☆ 250g (9oz) double (heavy) cream

☆ 60g (2¼oz) glucose

☆ 500g (1lb 2oz) milk, white or strawberry chocolate callets

chocolate fudge frosting

This is very definitely a favourite frosting for children, and is guaranteed to have them licking the topping off before they even start on the cake!

you will need...

☆ 100g (3½oz) unsalted butter, softened

☆ 500g (1lb 2oz) icing (confectioners') sugar

☆ 50g (1¾oz) cocoa powder (unsweetened cocoa)

☆ 6 tbsp (90ml) milk

☆ ½ tsp (2.5ml) vanilla extract

1 Place the butter in the bowl of an electric stand mixer and cream for 1–2 minutes. Meanwhile, sift the sugar and cocoa together into a separate bowl.

2 Add the milk, vanilla extract and half the sugar mixture to the butter and beat for at least 3 minutes, or until the mixture is light and fluffy.

3 Add the remaining sugar mixture and beat for a further 3 minutes, or until the mixture is light and fluffy and a spreadable consistency.

liquid fondant

If you don't want to use a buttercream frosting for any of the projects, or if you are looking for a dairy-free topping to accompany a dairy-free sponge, you can top your cakes with liquid fondant to give them a pristine, flat finish, onto which you can pop your decorated discs. The icing is crisp on the outside giving way to a soft fondant on the inside – think of those delightful French fancies from your childhood!

Fondant comes as a packet mix of icing (confectioners') sugar and glucose, so simply follow the manufacturer's instructions. The method usually involves mixing 2 teaspoons (10ml)

cooled boiled water to each 100g (3½oz) fondant to a stiff paste. Gently melt in a heatproof bowl set over a pan of hot water or in a double boiler, stirring continuously, then add a small amount of water for a glossy finish and heat to no more than 38°C (100°F), otherwise the icing will turn dull. Alternatively, use a microwave-safe bowl and heat in a microwave oven for bursts of 10–15 seconds, mixing in between to ensure that the icing doesn't overheat. Either spoon the fondant onto your cupcakes or pour it into a disposable plastic piping (pastry) bag and pipe directly into your cupcake case to flat fill (your cakes need to be level and not too high). If the fondant becomes too thick, simply pipe it back into the bowl and re-warm it.

techniques

Before you begin selecting the cupcake designs you want to create, it's worth taking a little time to review the main techniques involved, even if you're a practised cake decorator, to achieve a really professional finish and to learn some nifty new ways to bring extra personality and charm to your cupcake decorations.

applying frostings

Most of my cupcake designs have a buttercream or a frosting topping added before the final decoration. Check that your cupcakes are appropriate for the method of frosting – if they are too peaked or high, a flat finish won't work, so use a swirl of frosting instead, or re-bake with less mixture in the case!

All the cupcakes will taste great even if you choose to have some with just frosting on top for a more adult treat along with others that are fully decorated.

piping swirls

For beautiful swirls of frosting, it's well worth practising before piping for real. Cut the tip off a large disposable plastic piping (pastry) bag and drop your chosen piping tube (tip) into the bag. Always only half-fill the bag with the frosting so that it doesn't leak out. Eliminate any trapped air and then twist the open end of the bag closed, apply pressure and begin to pipe the frosting onto the cupcake.

1 Working from the outside inwards, pipe one complete swirl.

2 If you end up with too much of a peak of icing in the centre, tap the cupcake down sharply on the work surface.

flat-frosting

1 Take a full palette knife of frosting and spread around to fill the case (liner).

2 Then sweep the knife straight across the top of the cake, removing any excess, to give a completely flat top.

3 You can then place a sugarpaste disc directly on the flat surface, as in the Flame Cakes in Red Alert! (see Dressing Up).

piping a raised swirl

1 To create a cone shape of piped frosting, as featured in the Flame Cakes (see Dressing Up: Red Alert!), start near the centre of the cupcake and pipe upwards in a tight gradual spiral.

2 Build on the layer before to bring the frosting up to a peak.

3 To create a two-tone, marbled effect, as used for the same flame cupcake design, add alternate spoonfuls of two different frosting colours to the piping (pastry) bag.

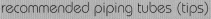

recommended piping tubes (tips)

no. 10 open star – great for piping a general swirl of frosting

no. 828 open star – for an alternative general swirl of frosting

no. 808 plain open round – great for piping no-fuss swirls of frosting

no. 1B drop (WIL) – used for creating the flame cakes (see Dressing Up: Red Alert!), and also good for simple roses: start at the centre and pipe outwards in spiral

using sugarpaste

You can make your own sugarpaste, but it's easiest to buy ready-made. For all the projects I have added CMC (carboxymethyl cellulose) to sugarpaste, a synthetic gum that adds elasticity and strength. This effectively turns it into modelling paste, which you can buy ready-prepared but it's preferable to add CMC to sugarpaste so that you can use pre-coloured pastes yet give them that extra flexibility and strength desirable for sugar decorations.

adding CMC to sugarpaste

To make up a batch of sugarpaste with CMC, use 1 tsp CMC per 225g (8oz) sugarpaste. Make a well in the sugarpaste and knead in the CMC. If using small amounts of different colours straight from the packet, just pick up a tiny amount of CMC on the end of a palette knife and knead in. The paste will start to firm as soon as the CMC is incorporated so that it can be used straight away. Knead it well before using to make it warmer and thus more pliable. It will continue to firm over the next day and then remain firm. Store the paste in a plastic bag.

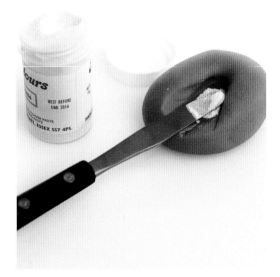

colouring sugarpaste

I tend to use commercially colour-mixed pastes, as they have been scientifically balanced not to be too dry or sticky to work with, but you can add colouring to white sugarpaste instead. Apply a gel paste colour with a cocktail stick (toothpick) so that you don't add too much colour at any one time, and use plastic gloves to stop the colour dyeing your hands bright green or red – you can get some funny looks when you forget to use gloves!

If making a dark colour, to prevent the paste turning sticky from the large amount of gel paste colour needed, add a pinch of CMC and leave the paste in a plastic bag for 10 minutes to firm a little.

colouring other icing

For colouring frostings, such as buttercream, I usually use gel paste colours. But remember to take into account the colour of your frosting, which can affect the colours you add to it, for example the natural pale yellow of buttercream will make a light red colour look quite orange or pink, or a blue colour take on a greenish tinge.

For colouring royal icing, use droplet food colours for making pale colours and gel paste colours for creating much deeper tones or black.

blending sugarpaste colours

To create a specific colour such as deep purple, you can start with a purple-coloured paste and add extra gel paste colour to it. However, I prefer to blend different pre-coloured pastes, such as purple and navy blue, which makes a really vibrant deep purple.

It's a good idea to experiment with blending colours, as it saves you having to stop and mix each individually — just take a pinch or ball of each colour such as red and yellow, then simply knead together and you have orange!

Creating flesh-coloured paste

Use the blending method to create different flesh tones for your decorations:

Girls peach-coloured paste for a rose complexion

Boys a soft beige made from teddy bear brown plus white

Mid-tone teddy bear brown plus chocolate

Darker tone chocolate brown

blended sugarpaste effects

You can also create fantastic special effects by blending colours, such as the swirly space background for the Spaced Out projects where purple and black are blended into navy blue, or the yellow and red blend for the fiery colour of the planets for the Celestial Sensation cupcakes.

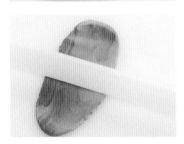

covering with sugarpaste

I love the look of sugarpaste (rolled fondant) placed directly onto cupcakes. Just follow these simple steps to ensure a neat, professional result.

1 Using a palette knife, apply a little buttercream directly to the sponge surface to adhere the paste.
2 Knead the sugarpaste until it is warm and flexible, then roll it out using a non-stick rolling pin on a non-stick work board (with a non-stick mat underneath to prevent slipping). Place icing spacers either side of the paste you are rolling and keep rolling until the pin is rolling on the spacers evenly and your icing will then be a level 3mm (⅛in) thickness.

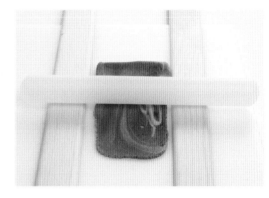

3 One of my most useful tools is a set of various sizes of circle cutter – select the most appropriate size for your cupcake and cut a circle.
4 Use a palette knife to lift the paste and place on top of your cupcake. Use the palm of your hand to smooth the paste into position. Trim off any excess with the palette knife if necessary.

creating features

You will be amazed how wide a variety of facial features and other details you can create by just using a few simple cutters to add character and individuality to your decorations.

making wings

The wings of the Busy Blackbirds featured in the Barnyard Fun chapter are created using an ordinary heart cutter.

1 Cut down once into the paste with a 3.5cm (1⅜in) heart cutter and lift the excess paste away.
2 Rotate the cutter slightly and cut down a second time so that you cut away some of the existing paste to create a three-pointed wing shape.

making sugar glue

You can buy sugar or edible glue for attaching features or decorations, but I love to make my own glue, as I can manage the consistency, creating a firm or looser glue depending on what I need to use it for. The synthetic gum CMC is used for this purpose too.

To make a batch of sugar glue, you need to make a blend of 1 part CMC to 20 parts warm, previously boiled water. Pick up the CMC on the end of a mini palette knife and place in a small screw-top jar. Add the water and stir. Leave with the lid off for 40 minutes to allow the glue to thicken. If you wish to make it the evening before, screw the lid on and leave in the fridge overnight to activate.

creating mouths

You can use different methods of making a mouth to bring variety to your sugar characters.

using a smile tool

Specialist smile tools are available that create perfect little smiles by simply pressing the tool into the paste. Both a ball tool and a smile tool (PME) are useful for impressing mouths and hollows in ears (see Techniques: Making Ears).

using a piping tube

For a larger smile or one at an angle, I love to use the open end of a fine piping tube (tip) pressed into the paste. You can then add definition by making an indentation with a cocktail stick (toothpick) at either end of the smile (see Spaced Out: Space Explorers).

using a heart cutter

To create a pursed look, use a mini heart plunger cutter to cut a tiny heart (see Dressing Up: Doctors & Nurses). You can also add the heart, cut from deep red or pink paste, as a detail to an impressed smile, which is ideal for giving a female character a cute look (see Fairytales & Adventure: Magical Mermaids).

using a straw

If you don't have any of these tools handy, a plastic drinking straw also works well. Just cut off the end at an angle and use to impress the paste.

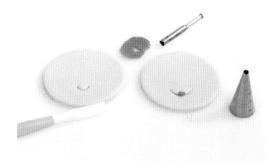

making eyes

There are so many ways to create eyes, and the following are the main techniques I've used in the book.

black eyes

The simplest method of making eyes is to use small black circles of paste. You can either cut these out with a mini circle plunger cutter; pipe them with a dot of black royal icing; use a black edible pen; use a cocktail stick (toothpick) dipped into black paste food colour; or roll pinches of black paste into tiny balls, flatten slightly and attach in place with sugar glue.

black and white eyes

Cut small circles of white paste and add a piped dot of black royal icing for pupils.

detailed eyes

Cut small circles or ovals of white paste and then use a blue edible pen to create the irises and a black edible pen to add the pupils.

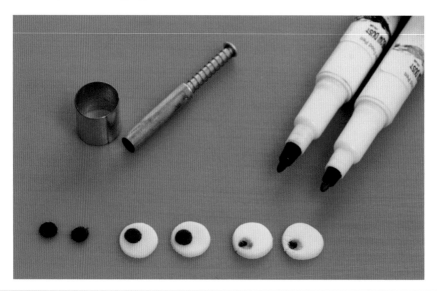

double heart eyes

For some of the animal designs in the Barnyard Fun chapter I've used two heart cutters of different sizes to cut one white paste heart and one pale blue, then overlapped them and cut through the base of both layers with the cutter chosen for the snout or muzzle. The latter then fits snugly up against the trimmed eyes. Black pupils are then added to the inner eyes.

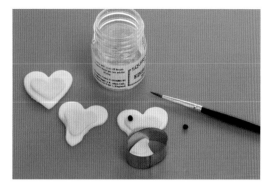

ready-made sugar eyes

Used for the aliens in the Alien Invasion cupcakes (see the Spaced Out chapter), these are available from sugarcraft stores or online suppliers. They give a great effect and will save you valuable time if you have lots of cupcakes to create.

For shiny eyes, add a dab of edible clear gel (see Techniques: Special Finishes).

making ears

I've used various ways to make ears in the projects, either for animals or people, but all using standard cutters.

easy animal ears

Use a 3.5cm (1⅜in) heart cutter to cut a single heart and then cut it in half vertically with a palette knife to make a pair of pointed ears. You can then turn the shapes upside down to create a different style of ear, as in Barnyard Fun: Playful Pups.

curled animal ears

Use a heart cutter to cut a heart from thinly rolled-out paste and then cut it in half vertically, but this time trim off the bottom third of the pointed end from each half, curl the two sides inwards and lightly pinch the rounded part. These are then attached to the animal's face horizontally, as in the Mooing Cows and Little Lambs projects (see Barnyard Fun).

two-tone animal ears

These ears are used for the Porky Piggies (see Barnyard Fun). Use the 3.5cm (1⅜in) heart cutter to cut two hearts from dark pink paste and then another two from light pink paste. With the points of the hearts pointing upwards, position the light pink shapes on top of the dark pink shapes, slightly lower down, to create inner ears. Cut across the hearts to trim off the rounded parts. After attaching the ears with sugar glue, you can curl them slightly to give them some character.

human ears

For one pair of ears, simply roll a ball of flesh-coloured paste (see Techniques: Using Sugarpaste), then impress a hollow with the small end of the ball tool. Cut in half, squeeze slightly and glue into position on either side of the character's face (see Dressing Up: Pop Idols).

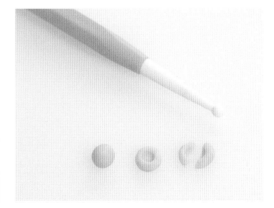

special finishes

It's easy to add extra wow factor to your sugar decorations by using a variety of finishes to create special light-catching effects.

lustre dusts

To give your decorations a gold or silver metallic finish, the first step is to create the item in either grey paste if you are going to paint it silver or in beige or teddy bear brown if you are going to use gold paint. The technique for mixing the dust solution will work with any dust colour whether plain or shimmering – simply use a mini spatula to place a small amount of dust onto a saucer or in a paint palette and add a little alcohol. You can use a regular white spirit such as gin or vodka, or use a specialist product called isopropyl alcohol. Add a little at a time and mix with a paintbrush until you have the desired consistency. As you paint with the mix the alcohol evaporates, so add a little more to maintain the right consistency.

sparkling effects

Edible shimmering flakes for decorating are available from specialist cake-decorating stores and online suppliers, along with non-toxic glitters. To add a touch of sparkle to your decorations, dip a dry, fluffy paintbrush (no. 8 pony) into the shimmering flakes and tap it above your cakes – do this sparingly for the best result. But for some details, such as the glasses for the Pop Idols cakes (see Dressing Up) or the fairy wands (see Fairytales & Adventure: Fabulous Fairies), total coverage is what you want. Simply paint the paste item, such as a star, completely with sugar glue and then tap the shimmering flakes above it until it is covered. Lift with a mini palette knife and tap off the excess above a piece of baking (parchment) paper – the excess flakes can then be returned to the pot.

edible clear gel

To create a realistic water effect or just to give some attractive shine to simple features such as eyes, add a touch of edible clear gel (piping jelly). It stays looking wet and will make your cupcake decorations extra glossy.

presentation & display

There are lots of exciting ways to present your decorated cupcakes, whether as an eye-catching display or for a special gift, so it's worth taking time to consider the various creative options.

cupcake wrappers

These are a simple way to add a bit of fun to your cupcakes, and there are designs and patterns available for every occasion.

cupcake stands

These look fantastic even before you add the cupcakes! Available as single layers or in tiers in a variety of designs and materials such as china, Perspex, wire or acrylic, they are perfect for creating a professional display at parties and special events.

single cupcake gift boxes

There are lots of individual cardboard cupcake boxes available with clear lids, as well as clear plastic boxes that can be dressed with colour-coordinating ribbon, which are ideal for when you want to present single cupcakes as a special gift or for guests to take home with them.

large cupcake gift boxes

Cardboard cupcake boxes have a tray with multiple holes cut into it for keeping the cupcakes in position and a clear lid, making them great for presenting a whole collection of cupcakes as a gift.

If serving your cupcakes on a platter, add a touch of decoration appropriate to the theme, such as some shredded coloured paper for a grass or nest effect, to set them off.

storage & transportation

Wherever possible I try to create decorations and even cupcakes ahead of time so that on the day I only have to whip up the frosting and put them all together. This isn't possible for every design in the book, but where you can it's the best approach to adopt, as it takes the stress out of the occasion and makes it all the more fun! Just take care and plan for storing and transporting your cupcakes.

storage containers

It's important to use the appropriate container to maintain your cakes and/or decorations in tip-top condition.

airtight plastic storage boxes

These are great for storing cupcakes if you bake them the night before, or even to freeze them in.

cardboard cupcake boxes

These are ideal for storing your decorated discs or decorations, as they allow a limited amount of air to circulate around them during the drying process while keeping them in a dust-free environment. Don't use plastic containers, as they cause the icing to sweat.

safe transit

If you need to transport your cupcakes, make sure you package them up in the right way to protect them and ensure that they arrive in perfect shape.

cardboard cupcake boxes

This is the very best way to transport your cupcakes, each having its own little hole to sit in so that the cakes don't slide around when on the move. You can stack the boxes to make them easy to carry.

plastic 'cupcake' caddies

Some varieties of these are stackable and have multi-layers that are great for transporting cakes.

When transporting your cupcake creations by road, use non-stick matting on the floor of the vehicle so that your cake box won't move around in transit.

barnyard fun

These cute animal characters are all created from simple heart, oval and circle cutters – just change the icing colours, twist the cutter and trim the cut-outs to vary the shapes, and suddenly you've created a whole farmful! You can bake your cakes and make the animal discs in advance, and then when you're ready, pipe on the buttercream and pop on your friendly farm-themed faces.

Note: For full sugarpaste amounts required in projects see Sugarpaste Quantities & Colourings section at end of book.

little lambs

The fluffy appearance of these lovely lambs is achieved by simply layering cut-out hearts. These are great for kids to make, as they love cutting out lots of shapes.

you will need...

makes 12

☆ 12 cupcakes piped with swirl of frosting

☆ sugarpaste (rolled fondant) with CMC (see Sugarpaste Quantities & Colourings)

☆ black royal icing in piping (pastry) bag with no. 1.5 piping tube (tip)

☆ 2cm (¾in) heart cutter

☆ smile tool

1 For the lamb body bases, roll out the white sugarpaste to 3mm (⅛in) thick using spacers. Use a circle cutter (no. 7) to cut 12 circles to fit your cupcakes.

2 To create one fluffy lamb coat, cut 11 hearts from the remaining white paste. Starting at the outer edge, arrange a layer of seven hearts on top of the body base with the points towards the centre. Arrange a second inner layer of the remaining four hearts on top.

3 For the head, roll a lozenge shape of black sugarpaste, place in the centre of the fluffy coat and check for sizing, then attach with sugar glue. For one pair of ears, roll out some black sugarpaste thinly and cut a heart. Cut in half vertically. Trim the pointed end from each half, curl the two sides inwards and lightly pinch the rounded part. Attach horizontally either side of the top of the head.

4 For one pair of eyes, roll two small balls of white paste and flatten slightly. Pipe on black royal icing pupils. Use a smile tool and cocktail stick (toothpick) to indent nostrils.

take care...

When working with black sugarpaste, make sure you use a separate work surface to avoid discolouring paler paste colours.

Recipes cupcake, topping *Techniques* applying frostings, using sugarpaste, creating features

porky piggies

Your barnyard scene needs some perfect pink pigs. You can vary the features to give them individual comic expressions and add melted chocolate mud splodges.

you will need...

makes 12

- ☆ 12 cupcakes piped with swirl of frosting
- ☆ sugarpaste (rolled fondant) with CMC (see Sugarpaste Quantities & Colourings)
- ☆ black royal icing in piping (pastry) bag with no. 1.5 piping tube (tip)
- ☆ cutters: 3.5cm (1⅜in) & 2cm (¾in) heart, 1.8cm (¾in) oval, mini circle plunger
- ☆ ball tool

1 For the faces, roll out the pale pink sugarpaste to 3mm (⅛in) thick using spacers. Use a circle cutter (no. 7) to cut 12 circles to fit your cupcakes.

2 For one pair of ears, from the thinly rolled-out sugarpaste, cut two large bright pink hearts and two pale pink hearts. With the points of the hearts pointing upwards, position the pale pink shapes on the bright pink shapes slightly lower down to create inner ears. Cut across the hearts to trim off the rounded parts. Attach to the top of the face with sugar glue. Curl the ears to give them movement.

3 For one pair of eyes, cut a large heart from thinly rolled-out white sugarpaste and a small heart from pale blue. Position the pale blue heart on top of the white, leaving a wide margin of white showing. Using the oval cutter, cut across the bottom of the hearts where the snout will sit.

4 For the snout, cut an oval from the remaining bright pink paste rolled out to 6mm (¼in) thick. Make indents for the nostrils with a ball tool.

5 Attach the eyes and snout with sugar glue. For the pupils, use the mini circle plunger cutter to cut black paste circles and attach. Pipe on the mouth with black royal icing, adding little curves at the ends.

mooing cows

Moove over – here come a whole herd of moo-cows! As well as being big, smiley personalities, they are strikingly marked with black patches.

you will need...

makes 12

☆ 12 cupcakes piped with swirl of frosting

☆ sugarpaste (rolled fondant) with CMC (see Sugarpaste Quantities & Colourings)

☆ black royal icing in piping (pastry) bag with no. 1.5 piping tube (tip)

☆ cutters: 3.5cm (1⅜in) & 2cm (¾in) heart, 1.8cm (¾in) oval, mini circle plunger

☆ ball tool

1 For the faces, roll out the white sugarpaste to 3mm (⅛in) thick using spacers. Use a circle cutter (no. 7) to cut 12 circles.

2 For one pair of markings, cut two large hearts from thinly rolled-out black sugarpaste. Trim off the bottom part of each and position the rounded part on either side of the face. Use the circle cutter from Step 1 to trim the edges. Attach with sugar glue.

3 For one pair of ears, cut a large heart from thinly rolled-out white paste. Cut in half vertically. Trim the pointed end from each half, curl the two sides inwards and lightly pinch the rounded part. Attach horizontally.

4 For the forelock, cut a rectangle of black sugarpaste and cut one edge in a deep zigzag with a knife. Use the back of the knife to score lines to create texture. Attach to the top centre of the face. For horns, roll a pea-size ball of white sugarpaste into a pointed sausage, then cut in half. Attach either side of the forelock.

5 Follow Porky Piggies: Step 3 to create the eyes (but swap the white and pale blue) and snout. For the pupils, use the mini circle plunger cutter to cut black paste circles and attach. Pipe on the mouth with black royal icing to one side of the face, adding little curves at the ends.

Recipes cupcake, topping   *Techniques* applying frostings, using sugarpaste, creating features

playful pups

The appealing hound-dog look of these barnyard puppies can be easily changed to a sheepdog – just use black and white sugarpaste and alter the ear shape.

you will need...
makes 12

- ☆ 12 cupcakes piped with swirl of frosting
- ☆ sugarpaste (rolled fondant) with CMC (see Sugarpaste Quantities & Colourings)
- ☆ cutters: 3.5cm (1⅜in) & 2cm (¾in) heart, 2.8cm (1in) oval, mini circle plunger
- ☆ smile tool

1 For the faces, roll out the caramel sugarpaste to 3mm (⅛in) thick using spacers. Use a circle cutter (no. 7) to cut 12 circles to fit your cupcakes.

2 For one pair of ears, cut out a large heart from the thinly rolled-out dark chocolate brown sugarpaste. Cut in half vertically to create two teardrop shapes. Attach to the face with sugar glue – either with the point at the top or partway down the face with the curve at the top and the tips curled. This will give you two different looks.

3 Follow Porky Piggies: Step 3 to create the eyes, but using a 2.8cm (1in) oval cutter to cut across the hearts where the muzzle will sit.

4 For the muzzle, cut an oval from cream sugarpaste rolled out to 3mm (⅛in) thick. Use a cocktail stick (toothpick) to indent holes for whiskers and a smile tool to create the mouth.

5 Attach the eyes and muzzle with sugar glue. For the pupils, use the mini circle plunger cutter to cut black paste circles and attach in place.

6 For the nose, roll a small ball of the dark chocolate sugarpaste and attach to the middle top of the muzzle with sugar glue.

Recipes cupcake, topping *Techniques* applying frostings, using sugarpaste, creating features

busy blackbirds

These beady-eyed birds can be found in fields of crops dodging scarecrows or flapping around the barnyard looking for grain. No wonder they now need a rest!

you will need...

makes 12

☆ 12 cupcakes piped with swirl of frosting

☆ sugarpaste (rolled fondant) with CMC (see Sugarpaste Quantities & Colourings)

☆ cutters: 3.5cm (1⅜in) & 2cm (¾in) heart, mini circle plunger

1 For the bodies, roll out the black sugarpaste to 3mm (⅛in) thick using spacers. Use a circle cutter (no. 7) to cut 12 circles.

2 For one pair of wings, roll out the black sugarpaste thinly. Use the large heart cutter to cut down once into the paste and lift the excess paste away. Rotate the cutter slightly and cut down a second time so that you cut away some of the existing paste to create a three-pointed wing shape. Repeat to cut a second wing.

3 For one pair of eyes, cut a small heart from thinly rolled-out white sugarpaste. Cut straight across to trim off the bottom pointed part. For the

beak, cut a large heart from thinly rolled-out bright yellow sugarpaste. Curl the two curved edges of the heart inwards and squeeze together, then trim the pointed end.

4 To make the bird look as if he is perched with his head nestling by his wings, position the eyes to the right-hand side of the body, with the feathers of one wing overhanging the left-hand side, then the second wing overlapping the first. Lay the beak on top of the end of the wings below the eyes. Attach all the pieces in place with sugar glue.

5 Plunger-cut two small black paste circles for pupils and attach.

Recipes cupcake, topping *Techniques* applying frostings, using sugarpaste, creating features

spaced out

Each of these out-of-this-world cupcake designs features the same space background – a swirly cosmic blend of dense sugarpaste colours that sets off the dazzling space motifs to perfection. The decorated cakes can then be enhanced with a sparkling finish for a super-spangly impact.

Note: For full sugarpaste amounts required in projects see Sugarpaste Quantities & Colourings section at end of book.

blast off!

A brightly coloured rocket soaring through outer space is a dynamic design to create – why not mix them with some of the star cakes (see Celestial Sensation) for them to zoom past?

you will need...

makes 12

- ☆ 12 cupcakes, flat-frosted
- ☆ sugarpaste (rolled fondant) and/with CMC (see Sugarpaste Quantities & Colourings)
- ☆ mini circle plunger cutter

1 For the space background, add a little of the teaspoon of CMC to each sugarpaste colour individually. Knead the colours separately until flexible and warm and then knead together until you get a swirly blend. Roll out to 3mm (⅛in) thick using spacers. Use a no. 8 circle cutter to cut 12 circles. Smooth onto the flat-frosted cakes and trim to fit.

2 For the body of the rocket, roll a sausage shape of white sugarpaste and then cut off the base with a knife and bring the other end to a point. Cut a strip of red sugarpaste and then wrap it around the point of the rocket a short distance from the tip.

3 For the flame, roll out the blended yellow and red sugarpaste and cut out a zigzag shape with your knife. Attach to the base of the rocket with sugar glue.

4 For the windows, use the mini circle plunger cutter to mark a small indentation on the body of each rocket just below the red ring.

5 For the fins, roll out the bright blue paste and cut three triangular shapes for each rocket. Attach in place, one laid flat either side of the rocket body and one vertically down the centre, extending beyond the rocket base.

Recipes cupcake, topping *Techniques* applying frostings, using sugarpaste

space explorers

These intrepid spacemen certainly look happy enough to be exploring new worlds out in the star-studded universe. Make your own choice of complexion by blending a particular flesh tone.

you will need...
makes 12

- ☆ 12 cupcakes, flat-frosted
- ☆ sugarpaste (rolled fondant) and/with CMC (see Sugarpaste Quantities & Colourings)
- ☆ gold lustre dust & edible shimmering flakes
- ☆ cutters: 2.8cm (1in) & 4cm (1½in) oval, 1.4cm (⅝in) circle, mini circle/star plunger
- ☆ no. 2 piping tube (tip)

1 Cover the cupcakes with the space background (see Blast Off!: Step 1).

2 Using cutters, roll out the flesh paste very thinly and cut a small oval for the face. For the helmet, roll out the white paste thinly and cut a large oval. Cut out the centre using the smaller cutter. Place the face inside the helmet and smooth with your fingers to fit snugly.

3 For the smile, use the open end of the piping tube to make an impression, then a cocktail stick (toothpick) to make a small indentation at either end. Use the narrow end of the tube to impress rivets around the helmet.

4 For one pair of ear covers, cut a white paste circle with the small circle cutter and cut in half. Stick either side of the helmet with sugar glue. Roll a small ball of flesh paste for the nose and plunger-cut mini black paste circles for the eyes. Attach in place.

5 For the spacesuit, roll three sausages of white paste graduating in size and flatten slightly. Position beneath the helmet, then flatten and smooth them to blend together.

6 Make and attach a star to each cake (see Celestial Sensation: Step 2). Using a no. 8 pony paintbrush, sprinkle the cakes with edible shimmering flakes.

Recipes cupcake, topping *Techniques* applying frostings, using sugarpaste, creating features, special finishes

celestial sensation

Dot these glowing stars and planets around your other space cakes to create a collection. For a party solution, combine just a couple of astronauts and rockets with lots of these quick designs.

you will need...

makes 12

- ☆ 12 cupcakes, flat-frosted
- ☆ sugarpaste (rolled fondant) and/with CMC (see Sugarpaste Quantities & Colourings)
- ☆ gold lustre dust
- ☆ silver dragées (sugar balls)
- ☆ edible shimmering flakes
- ☆ dusting brush
- ☆ star plunger cutter set (PME)

1 Cover the cupcakes with the space background (see Blast Off!: Step 1).

2 For the stars, roll out the yellow paste thinly, then use a dusting brush to dust the surface with gold lustre dust. Use the plunger cutter from the set to cut stars in a variety of sizes.

3 For the planets, roll out the blended yellow and red paste thinly. Use a circle cutter of your choice (I used a no. 2 here) to cut out six planets and attach with sugar glue to half the cupcakes. To indicate that the planets are in orbit, roll a fine rope of black sugarpaste, loop around each planet and attach.

4 Add a couple of stars to each planet cake, then push some dragées into the icing. Arrange and attach a selection of different-size stars to the star cakes, then add some dragées. Finish by sprinkling over edible shimmering flakes with a no. 8 pony paintbrush.

colour your planet...
The yellow and red blend creates a lovely fiery effect, but you could try other colour blends such as purples, blues, greens or browns.

Recipes cupcake, topping, *Techniques* applying frostings, using sugarpaste, special finishes

alien invasion

There's nothing to fear from these invading aliens — they look very friendly, and kids will love their three goggly eyes and spaceships studded with colourful candy-coated chocolate sweets.

you will need...

makes 12

- ☆ 12 cupcakes, flat-frosted
- ☆ sugarpaste (rolled fondant) and/with CMC (see Sugarpaste Quantities & Colourings)
- ☆ 48 candy-coated chocolate sweets (candies)
- ☆ ready-made sugar eyes
- ☆ edible shimmering flakes
- ☆ 1.5 piping tube (tip)

1 Cover the cupcakes with the space background (see Blast Off!: Step 1).

2 For the spaceship, roll out the white sugarpaste to 3mm (⅛in) thick using spacers. Use the largest cutter from the circle cutter set to cut a circle. Use the same cutter to cut about 1.5cm (⅝in) inside the outer edge for the outer part of the spaceship, then trim the ends. For the bubble part where the alien sits, use the no. 4 circle cutter to cut a circle, then use the largest cutter to trim off the bottom third of the circle. Position the two parts together on the cake.

3 For the alien, roll an 8g (¼oz) ball of the lime green paste into an oval shape and flatten slightly with your fingers into place to make a head. Roll another smaller ball to form the top part of the body and smooth into place, trimming if required. Roll a teardrop shape, then use your fingers to smooth into a trumpet-shaped horn (or why not create lots!) and insert the handle of a paintbrush into the end. Attach to the head.

4 For the smile, use the open end of the piping tube to indent a curve and then a cocktail stick (toothpick) at either end to give it definition.

5 Stick the sweets and edible eyes in place, then sprinkle the cakes with edible shimmering flakes.

Recipes cupcake, topping   *Techniques* applying frostings, using sugarpaste, creating features, special finishes

red alert!

Your brave unit of pretend firefighting recruits have everything they need here to set the scene – and to douse those threatening flames of hunger!

you will need...
makes 12

☆ 12 cupcakes, 4 flat-frosted

☆ sugarpaste (rolled fondant) with CMC (see Sugarpaste Quantities & Colourings)

☆ vanilla buttercream: ½ smaller quantity each Melon Yellow (SF)-coloured & Red Extra (SF)-coloured

☆ mini star plunger cutter

☆ no. 1B drop (WIL) piping tube (tip)

for the fire hose cakes

1 For the bases, roll out the yellow paste to 3mm (⅛in) thick using spacers. Use the no. 6 circle cutter to cut four discs. Set aside to firm.

2 For a hose, roll a long rope of red paste, using an icing smoother to roll evenly. Coil around on the centre of a yellow disc to create a neat mound, leaving the end trailing down the front. For the nozzle, roll a small sausage of grey paste and then roll it more in the centre to make an hourglass shape. Push the end of a paintbrush into the nozzle to create an open end. Attach with sugar glue.

just add water...
To create a water effect, add edible clear gel dotted about at the end of the fire hose.

Recipes cupcake, topping   Techniques applying frostings, using sugarpaste

for the firefighter's helmet cakes

1 For the bases, roll out the red paste to 3mm (⅛in) thick using spacers. Use the no. 6 circle cutter to cut four discs. Set aside to firm.

2 For each helmet, roll 15g (½oz) of the yellow paste into a ball. Shape with your fingers into a helmet shape. Cut a thick strip of the yellow paste and attach it down the centre of the helmet, running from the brim at the front over the crown to the brim at the rear.

3 To complete the helmets, use the plunger cutter to cut small stars from red paste. Attach a star to the front of each helmet, positioning it on the central strip.

for the flame cakes

1 For the bases, roll out the blended yellow and red paste to 3mm (⅛in) thick using spacers. Use a no. 8 circle cutter to cut four discs. Smooth onto the flat-frosted cakes and trim to fit.

2 Place alternate spoonfuls of the yellow- and red-coloured buttercreams into a disposable plastic piping (pastry) bag fitted with the piping tube. Starting in the centre of the sugarpaste top and keeping close to the centre, pipe a tall coil of the marbled buttercream onto each cake.

to finish the fire hose & firefighter's helmet cakes

1 Use the remaining marbled buttercream to pipe a swirl onto each unfrosted cupcake.

2 Top with the decorated discs.

cops & robbers

Every child loves playing police chase, racing around with a toy squad car, so here are the cakes to match the action, complete with emergency cones and handcuffs to corner and catch the baddies!

you will need...
makes 12

☆ 12 cupcakes piped with swirl of frosting

☆ sugarpaste (rolled fondant) with CMC (see Sugarpaste Quantities & Colourings)

☆ silver lustre dust mixed with alcohol

☆ silver dragées (sugar balls)

☆ cutters: car set with window and wheel (C4F), mini circle plunger

For the bases, roll out the navy blue paste to 3mm (⅛in) thick using spacers. Use a no. 6 circle cutter to cut 12 discs. Set aside to firm.

for the police car cakes

1 Use the car cutter set to cut four car shapes from white paste. Cut out the windows, reversing the cutter to cut the second window. Cut out two half-wheel shapes from each car. Position each car on a navy blue disc.

2 Cut thin strips of yellow and blue paste. Lay the strips side by side and cut across the strips to create squares. Attach the squares to each car in a strip of alternating colours.

3 For the police light, roll a small ball of blue paste and trim to create a flat edge. Attach to the car roof. Cut wheels from black paste and ease into place. Use the plunger cutter to cut yellow wheel centres and attach.

Recipes cupcake, topping Techniques applying frostings, using sugarpaste, special finishes

for the emergency cone cakes

1 Roll out the white paste thinly. Cut two narrow strips and lay horizontally a short distance apart on the rolled-out orange paste. Use a palette knife to cut out four horizontally striped triangles.

2 Remove any white paste from the excess orange paste, then roll it out again but this time fairly thickly. Cut a strip for each cone and attach to the bottom to form a base.

scene of the crime...
Make lots of these simple cakes and use to cordon off the party food and set the action-packed scene!

for the handcuff cakes

1 For each set of handcuffs, cut a circle from the thinly rolled-out blended grey paste using a no. 2 circle cutter, then cut out an inner circle from it using a no. 4 circle cutter. Lift the ring onto a navy blue disc and arrange to create an oval. Repeat to cut a second ring and lay overlapping the first ring.

2 Cut a narrow strip of grey paste and lay across the bottom of the rings to link them. Indent a series of holes in the link with the end of a paintbrush. Paint the handcuffs with the silver lustre dust solution.

3 Using a paintbrush, dab sugar glue into each indentation and then press a silver dragée into each hollow.

super troopers

Turn the party into a successful campaign with these atmospheric army-themed cupcakes, featuring young soldiers complete with convincing camouflage helmets and mud-splotched faces.

you will need...
makes 12

- ☆ 12 cupcakes, 8 piped with swirl of frosting
- ☆ sugarpaste (rolled fondant) with CMC (see Sugarpaste Quantities & Colourings)
- ☆ silver lustre dust mixed with alcohol
- ☆ no. 1.5 piping tube (tip)
- ☆ cutters: mini circle plunger, star to fit no. 3 circle cutter
- ☆ cleaned toy vehicle with deep treads

for the soldier cakes

1 For the faces, roll out the flesh-coloured paste to 3mm (⅛in) thick using spacers. Use a no. 6 circle cutter to cut four discs. While soft, impress a smile on each using the open end of the piping tube and then indent at either end with a cocktail stick (toothpick).

2 For the helmets, knead the dark bottle green, teddy bear brown, chocolate brown and light green pastes separately, tear into pieces and roll into little balls. Put the balls together into one lump and cut through into two pieces. Roll out each piece and use the no. 6 circle cutter to cut two circles. Cut in half, then arch the bottom edge of each semicircle to create a brim. Attach the helmets to the faces.

frosting for combat...
To camouflage your frosting, colour vanilla buttercream green and spoon into the piping (pastry) bag alternating with chocolate frosting.

Recipes cupcake, topping *Techniques* applying frostings, using sugarpaste, creating features, special finishes

3 For the chin straps, cut long strips of the camouflage paste and attach in place.

4 For eyes, cut white paste circles with the mini circle plunger cutter and attach. Flatten tiny balls of black paste slightly and add for pupils. For the nose, roll a tiny ball of the flesh-coloured paste and attach.

5 Wet a little dark green or brown paste to make a sticky paint. Dab onto the faces with a paintbrush to create the effect of mud splotches.

for the medal cakes

1 For the bases, roll out the chocolate brown paste to 3mm (⅛in) thick using spacers. Use a no. 6 circle cutter to cut four discs. Set aside to firm.

2 Roll out the grey paste and use a no. 3 circle cutter to cut four discs. Roll the remaining grey paste more thinly and cut four stars. Paint with the silver lustre dust solution and attach to the discs.

3 Roll out the red paste and cut a strip 4cm (1½in) wide, then roll very thinly and cut a strip 5mm (¼in) wide. Cut a very thin strip 2cm (¾in) wide of navy blue paste and a strip 1cm (½in) wide of white paste. Layer as shown in the photo. Trim a section of ribbon to fit above each medal.

for the tank track cakes

1 Roll out the chocolate brown sugarpaste to 3mm (⅛in) thick using spacers. Use the toy to indent tracks across the paste.

2 Push the green paste through a sieve (strainer) and place clumps here and there beside the tracks. Use the no. 8 circle cutter to cut out four discs from the paste and place on top of the remaining cakes (flat-frosted beforehand).

doctors & nurses

For another ever-popular children's dressing-up game, this little collection of medical staff and first-aid cupcakes is bound to make everyone feel a whole lot better!

you will need...

makes 12

- ☆ 12 cupcakes piped with swirl of frosting
- ☆ sugarpaste (rolled fondant) with CMC (see Sugarpaste Quantities & Colourings)
- ☆ cutters: 4cm (1½in) & 2cm (¾in) square, mini circle & heart plunger
- ☆ Dresden tool (optional)
- ☆ edible pens: blue, black
- ☆ ball tool

for the cross and plaster cakes

1 For the bases, roll out the pale blue paste or white paste to 3mm (⅛in) thick using spacers. Use a no. 6 circle cutter to cut four discs. Set aside to firm.

2 For the crosses, roll out the red sugarpaste thinly. Use the larger square cutter to cut two squares and then to cut away each corner. Attach each to a blue or white disc.

3 For the plasters, cut two strips 2cm x 5cm (¾in x 2in) from the thinly rolled-out pinkish brown paste and round off the ends, then use the small square cutter to cut two squares. Place each square in the centre of a disc, top with a strip and then score down either side of the square with a mini palette knife.

4 Use a cocktail stick (toothpick) to imprint the two end sections of the plaster with rows of dots, alternating the positioning of the dots from one row to the next.

Recipes cupcake, topping *Techniques* applying frostings, using sugarpaste, creating features

for the nurse cakes

1 For the faces, follow Cross and Plaster Cakes: Step 1 using the flesh-coloured (peach) paste.

2 For the hair, roll out the chocolate brown sugarpaste and use the no. 6 circle cutter to cut a circle. Use a palette knife or Dresden tool to trim the circle to create the hairline and then impress it with strokes of the knife or tool to give the impression of hair. Attach to the peach discs with sugar glue.

3 For the nose, roll a small ball of peach paste and attach to the face. For the eyes, use the mini circle plunger cutter to cut two small circles from white paste, then roll two tiny balls of black paste for pupils. Attach in place.

4 For the cap, roll out the remaining white paste and use a no. 11 circle cutter to cut a large circle, then cut through the circle with the cutter about halfway to create a band. Hold against the head, trim the ends to length and then attach. Use the small square cutter to cut a square of red paste, trim to size and then use the cutter to cut away each corner to form a cross. Attach to the cap front.

5 For the pursed mouth, use the mini heart plunger cutter to cut a heart from the remaining red paste and attach in place.

for the doctor cakes

1 For the faces, follow Cross and Plaster Cakes: Step 1 using the flesh-coloured (chocolate and teddy bear brown) paste.

2 For the surgical cap, use the no. 6 circle cutter to cut a green paste circle. Cut off the top portion in a curve with a sweeping stroke of the palette knife. Attach to the face.

3 For the eyes, use the mini circle plunger cutter to cut two small circles of white paste. Draw a circle in each eye with the blue edible pen to make the irises and then use the black edible pen to add the pupils. Attach in place.

4 For one pair of ears, roll a small ball of the flesh-coloured paste, then impress a hollow with the small end of the ball tool. Cut in half and glue each ear into position.

5 For the surgical mask, roll out the remaining green paste and cut a curved oblong shape with your palette knife. Roll two small strands of green paste and loop over the ears, then attach the mask in place.

pop idols

These show-stopping cupcakes are for all those youngsters who have stars in their eyes – just like our pop singer here depicted mid-performance. And every pop star needs some music and a mic!

you will need...
makes 12

- ☆ 12 cupcakes piped with swirl of frosting
- ☆ sugarpaste (rolled fondant) with CMC (see Sugarpaste Quantities & Colourings)
- ☆ silver lustre dust mixed with alcohol
- ☆ cutters: star plunger set, music and sports Tappit set (FMM), large star to fit no. 6 circle cutter
- ☆ ball tool

for the pop singer cakes

1 For the faces, roll out the flesh-coloured paste to 3mm (⅛in) thick using spacers. Use a no. 6 circle cutter to cut four discs.

2 For the nose, roll a small ball of the paste and attach. For one pair of ears, roll a larger ball, then impress a hollow with the small end of the ball tool. Cut in half and glue into position.

3 For the glasses, use the largest star cutter from the plunger cutter set to cut two stars from yellow sugarpaste and then lift into place. Roll two small strands of purple

paste and attach between the glasses and the ears.

4 For the hair, roll ropes of yellow sugarpaste tapering to a point. Glue the ends together at the forehead.

5 For the mouth, flatten a ball of black paste into an oval and attach to the face at a slight angle to look like he is singing.

added glitz and glamour...
To give the glasses sparkle, paint with gold lustre dust mixed with alcohol or sprinkle with gold edible shimmering flakes or non-toxic glitter.

Recipes cupcake, topping *Techniques* applying frostings, using sugarpaste, creating features, special finishes

for the musical note cakes

1 For the bases, roll out the purple paste to 3mm (⅛in) thick using spacers. Use a no. 6 circle cutter to cut four discs. Set aside to firm.

2 Using the Tappit set, cut two sets of musical notes from the thinly rolled-out yellow sugarpaste for each purple disc. Attach the notes to the centre of each disc.

the simple solution…
This quick and easy design is a great way to cater for a large number of party guests.

for the microphone cakes

1 For the bases, roll out the purple paste to 3mm (⅛in) thick using spacers. Use a no. 6 circle cutter to cut four discs. Set aside to firm.

2 Use the large star cutter to cut four stars from the thinly rolled-out yellow sugarpaste and attach one to the centre of each purple disc.

3 For the microphone handle, roll a tapering sausage of grey paste and trim the bottom flat. Cut a small strip of grey paste and attach down the centre as an on/off switch. Paint with the silver lustre dust solution.

4 For the microphone head, roll a ball of black sugarpaste slightly wider than the microphone handle and then flatten the base.

5 Attach a microphone handle to each yellow star with sugar glue and then attach the microphone heads in place.

Fairytales & adventure

Step into the enchanting world of make-believe with these fantasy cupcake designs based on ever-popular themes. Choose from the perils of thieving pirates and the thrills of fearless knights of old, or the bewitching charms of beautiful fairy princesses and mermaids. Each will weave their special magic to make an occasion truly memorable.

Note: For full sugarpaste amounts required in projects see Sugarpaste Quantities & Colourings section at end of book.

wicked pirates

These girl and boy pirate cakes, together with stolen treasure minis, are so much fun to create – you could hide them around the party venue and set the kids off on a treasure hunt to find them!

you will need...

makes 9

- ☆ 9 cupcakes piped with swirl of frosting
- ☆ sugarpaste (rolled fondant) with CMC (see Sugarpaste Quantities & Colourings)
- ☆ dragées (sugar balls)
- ☆ 1.5 piping tube (tip)
- ☆ cutters: 2cm (¾in) heart, mini circle & heart plunger, 1.4cm (⅝in) circle
- ☆ black edible pen
- ☆ ball tool

Use one of the cupcake recipes to bake nine standard cupcakes for the pirate cakes and about six mini cupcakes for the mini treasure cakes.

for the pirate cakes

1 For the faces, roll out the flesh-coloured pastes to 3mm (⅛in) thick using spacers. Use a no. 6 circle cutter to cut a mixture of nine discs.

2 While soft, impress a smile on each face using the open end of the piping tube (tip) and indent at either end with a cocktail stick (toothpick).

3 For two headscarves, roll out the red or pink paste to medium thickness and use the no. 6 circle cutter to cut a circle, then cut in

half. Cut across the bottom of each semicircle and smooth the edge.

4 For one headscarf tie, use the heart cutter to cut a red or pink heart, then cut in half lengthways. Pinch the curved part of each half. Attach together to one side of the scarf. Add a small ball of paste to the join.

5 For the spots, use the mini circle plunger cutter to cut lots of white paste circles, then gently flatten with your finger so that they are all slightly softened and different sizes. Attach to the scarf.

6 For the eyes, roll small balls of white paste, flatten slightly and attach two to the girls' faces and

---

one to the boys' faces. Use the mini circle plunger cutter to cut black paste pupils for each, or roll tiny balls and flatten slightly. Use a black edible pen to add eyelashes to the girls' eyes.

7 For the noses, roll small balls of flesh-coloured paste and attach.

8 For the girls' ears, roll a small ball of flesh paste, then impress a hollow with the small end of the ball tool. Cut in half and glue one half to the left-hand side of a face. Add a dragée for an earring.

9 Use the mini heart plunger to cut tiny red paste hearts. Attach to the centre of each girl's smile.

10 Use a cocktail stick (toothpick) to indent holes on the boys' chins for stubble and use the black edible pen to add a scar.

11 For the eyepatch, use the 1.4cm (⅝in) circle cutter to cut a black paste circle or roll a ball of black paste and flatten it. Trim off the top part and attach in place. Cut a narrow strip of the paste and glue over the headscarf for a strap.

the personal touch...
Vary the drawn-on details for each pirate to give them individual personality.

you will need...

makes 6 mini

☆ 6 mini cupcakes
piped with swirl of
whipped chocolate
frosting

☆ 6 gold foil-wrapped
chocolate coins

for mini treasure cakes

Top each mini cupcake
piped with a swirl of
chocolate frosting with
a gold foil-wrapped
chocolate coin.

magical mermaids

These ultra-glamorous mermaids have swirling tendrils of rich brown hair decorated with dragées to look like seed pearls.

you will need...

makes 9

- ☆ 9 cupcakes piped with swirl of frosting
- ☆ sugarpaste (rolled fondant) with CMC (see Sugarpaste Quantities & Colourings)
- ☆ pearl dragées (sugar balls)
- ☆ no. 1.5 piping tube (tip)
- ☆ mini heart plunger cutter
- ☆ edible pens: blue, black
- ☆ Dresden tool

Use one of the cupcake recipes to bake nine standard cupcakes for the mermaid cakes and about six mini cupcakes for the mini octopus cakes.

for the mermaid cakes

1 For the faces, roll out the flesh-coloured paste to 3mm (⅛in) thick using spacers. Use a no. 6 circle cutter to cut nine discs.

2 While soft, impress a smile on each face using the open end of the piping tube, positioning it to the left-hand side of the face. Indent at either end with a cocktail stick (toothpick). Plunger-cut tiny bright pink paste hearts. Attach to each mermaid's smile.

3 For the eyes, roll small white paste balls and flatten slightly. Use a blue and black edible pen to add irises, pupils and eyelashes.

4 For the hair, roll teardrops of the brown paste into fine ropes tapering to a point. Roll flat with a rolling pin and use the back of a Dresden tool to texture. Glue in place, some overlapping, and allow to flow outwards. Dot with pearl dragées.

super seashells...
Use a mini shell mould (DP) to create sugar shells for decorating the party table or a pretty crown for your mermaid, as pictured.

Recipes cupcake, topping   *Techniques* applying frostings, using sugarpaste, creating features

you will need...

makes 6 mini

- ☆ **6 mini cupcakes piped with swirl of frosting**
- ☆ **sugarpaste (rolled fondant) with CMC (see Sugarpaste Quantities & Colourings)**
- ☆ **smile tool**
- ☆ **black edible pen**

for the mini octopus cakes

1 For the bases, knead 35g (1¼oz) of the white and the pale blue pastes separately until flexible and warm, then knead together until you get a swirly blend. Roll out to 3mm (⅛in) thick using spacers and use a circle cutter to cut six discs to fit your mini cupcakes. Set aside to firm.

2 For the octopus, roll a large ball of yellow paste, then roll at an angle to create a teardrop shape with a tapered end. Using a knife, make two cuts starting a third of the way from the rounded end down to the tapered end, then cut in between to create eight sections. Roll each gently into a slim, tapering tentacle. Sit on the sugarpaste disc, curling, twisting and overlapping the tentacles.

3 For the head, indent a smile with the smile tool. Flatten two small white paste balls slightly into ovals for eyes. Attach in place. Add oval pupils with the black edible pen.

ocean wave frosting...
To create the sea blue-tinted frosting, colour a small amount of vanilla buttercream blue, smear it around your piping (pastry) bag with a palette knife, then add more plain buttercream.

fabulous fairies

You can tell that these are no ordinary fairies, with their silver crowns studded with precious 'pearls' and magical wands. There's lots of fun to be had here trying out different hairstyles for them.

you will need...

makes 9

- ☆ 9 cupcakes piped with swirl of frosting
- ☆ sugarpaste (rolled fondant) with CMC (see Sugarpaste Quantities & Colourings)
- ☆ silver pearl dragées
- ☆ silver lustre dust mixed with alcohol
- ☆ 1.5 piping tube (tip)
- ☆ mini heart plunger cutter
- ☆ edible pens: blue, black
- ☆ gun with hair disc

Use one of the cupcake recipes to bake nine standard cupcakes for the fairy cakes and about six mini cupcakes for the mini wand cakes.

for the fairy cakes

1 For the faces, roll out the flesh-coloured paste to 3mm (⅛in) thick using spacers. Use a no. 6 circle cutter to cut nine discs.

2 While soft, impress a smile on each face using the open end of the piping tube and indent at either end with a cocktail stick (toothpick). Use the mini heart plunger cutter to cut tiny bright pink paste hearts. Attach one to each fairy's smile.

3 For the eyes, roll small balls of white paste and flatten slightly. Use a blue edible pen to add irises and a black edible pen for pupils. Attach in place. Use the black edible pen to add eyelashes.

4 For the hair, knead the yellow paste and add a little sugar glue and white vegetable fat (shortening) until very soft. Push some of the paste into the sugarcraft gun and, using the handle, ease out tendrils of hair. Lift sections on a palette knife and attach with a touch of sugar glue. The hair can be plaited (braided) or left flowing and a fringe (bang) added.

Recipes cupcake, topping   *Techniques* applying frostings, using sugarpaste, creating features, special finishes

5 For the crown, use your palette knife to cut a crown shape with three points from grey paste. Paint with the silver lustre dust solution. Glue three pearl dragées to the base of the crown, then attach to the fairy.

glam her up…
To make your fairy princesses' hair even more gorgeous, create a decorative tie by cutting a lilac blossom using a mini blossom plunger cutter and adding a pearl dragée to the centre.

you will need...

makes 6 mini

☆ 6 mini cupcakes piped with swirl of frosting

☆ sugarpaste (rolled fondant) with CMC (see Sugarpaste Quantities & Colourings)

☆ 2.5cm (1in) star cutter

for the mini wand cakes

1 For the bases, roll out lilac sugarpaste with CMC to 3mm (⅛in) thick using spacers and use a circle cutter to cut six discs to fit the mini cakes. Set aside to firm.

2 For the wands, use the star cutter to cut stars from yellow paste. For the shafts, roll a long, narrow sausage of pink paste, then cut into lengths. Glue a shaft to each star onto each lilac disc.

wonder wands...
To add a sparkling finish to your fairy wands, paint the yellow stars with sugar glue and sprinkle with gold edible shimmering flakes or non-toxic glitter.

gallant knights

Every daring knight needs a fantastic helmet and demon sword to do fearless battle with dragons, and these sugar versions are sure to win the day.

you will need...

makes 9

- ☆ 9 cupcakes piped with swirl of frosting
- ☆ sugarpaste (rolled fondant) with CMC (see Sugarpaste Quantities & Colourings)
- ☆ no. 1.5 piping tube (tip)
- ☆ mini circle plunger cutter

Use one of the cupcake recipes to bake nine standard cupcakes for the knight cakes and about six mini cupcakes for the mini sword cakes.

for the knight cakes

1 For the faces, roll out the flesh-coloured paste to 3mm (⅛in) thick using spacers. Use a no. 6 circle cutter to cut nine discs. Set aside for them to firm.

2 For the helmet, roll out the grey paste and use the no. 6 circle cutter to cut a circle. Using the same cutter, cut away the lower portion in two sections either side, as shown in the photo, to create two curves that meet

in a 'V' at the centre. Use a palette knife to score a line down the centre and use the piping tube to indent a row of rivets either side.

3 For the feather holder, roll a small ball of grey paste, place it on your board and then use your fingers either side of it to roll and elongate it slightly. Use the end of a paintbrush to make a hole for the feather. Attach to the top of the helmet with sugar glue.

4 For the feather, roll a little red paste and elongate the end to create a teardrop shape, then flatten. Use your palette knife to

---

Recipes cupcake, topping   *Techniques* applying frostings, using sugarpaste, creating features

make cuts down the shape to feather it. Pinch the base into a stalk and push into the feather holder. Glue in place. Curl the feather plumes for a realistic effect.

5 For the visor, cut a 'V'-shape strip of grey paste to sit high up on the knight's face so that only his eyes will be showing. Use the piping tube to indent rivets around all the edges. For the slits, cut seven short narrow strips of black paste and attach vertically at even intervals to the visor.

6 For the eyes, use the mini circle plunger cutter to cut white paste circles and attach to the face. For the pupils, roll tiny balls of black paste, flatten slightly and use a moist paintbrush to pick up and attach in place.

contrasting colours...
Why not make just half of your knights' feathers red and the other half a different colour for an opposing army?

you will need...

makes 6 mini

☆ 6 mini cupcakes piped with swirl of frosting

☆ sugarpaste (rolled fondant) with CMC (see Sugarpaste Quantities & Colourings)

☆ 2cm (¾in) square cutter

for the mini sword cakes

1 For the bases, roll out the black paste to 3mm (⅛in) thick using spacers and use a circle cutter to cut six discs to fit the mini cakes. Set aside to firm.

2 For the sword blade, use your palette knife to cut a wide strip of grey paste, then trim the end to a point. Indent a line down the centre.

3 For the hilt, use the square cutter to cut a square of red paste, then cut away the bottom two corners with the cutter to create a 'T' shape. Use the piping tube to indent a row of rivets across the hilt. Glue the blades and hilts to the black discs.

barnyard fun

little lambs
Sugarpaste (rolled fondant) with CMC: 375g (13oz) white; 100g (3½oz) black

porky piggies
Sugarpaste (rolled fondant) with CMC: 250g (9oz) pale pink; 100g (3½oz) bright pink; a little white, pale blue and black

mooing cows
Sugarpaste (rolled fondant) with CMC: 300g (10½oz) white; 100g (3½oz) black; a little pale blue and bright pink

playful pups
Sugarpaste (rolled fondant) with CMC: 250g (9oz) caramel brown; 100g (3½oz) dark chocolate brown; a little white, pale blue and black; 50g (1¾oz) cream

busy blackbirds
Sugarpaste (rolled fondant) with CMC: 300g (10½oz) black; 50g (1¾oz) white; 50g (1¾oz) bright yellow

spaced out

blast off!
space background
Sugarpaste (rolled fondant): 175g (6oz) navy; 50g (1¾oz) purple; 25g (1oz) black; plus 1 tsp CMC

space rockets
Sugarpaste (rolled fondant) with CMC: 150g (5½oz) white; 10g (¼oz) red; 25g (1oz) yellow and 15g (½oz) red blended together; 100g (3½oz) bright blue

space explorers
space background
Sugarpaste (rolled fondant): 175g (6oz) navy, 50g (1¾oz) purple, 25g (1oz) black; plus 1 tsp CMC

spacemen
Sugarpaste (rolled fondant) with CMC: 40g (1½oz) flesh-coloured (see Techniques: Using

Sugarpaste); 150g (5½oz) white; 20g (¾oz) black; 10g (¼oz) yellow

celestial sensation
space background
Sugarpaste (rolled fondant): 175g (6oz) navy; 50g (1¾oz) purple; 25g (1oz) black; plus 1 tsp CMC

stars & planets
Sugarpaste (rolled fondant) with CMC: 20g (¾oz) yellow; 25g (1oz) yellow and 15g (½oz) red blended together; 20g (¾oz) black

alien invasion
space background
Sugarpaste (rolled fondant): 175g (6oz) navy; 50g (1¾oz) purple; 25g (1oz) black; plus 1 tsp CMC

spaceships & aliens
Sugarpaste (rolled fondant) with CMC: 250g (9oz) white; 130g (4½oz) lime green

dressing up

red alert!

fire hose cakes
Sugarpaste (rolled fondant) with CMC: 60g (2¼oz) Melon Yellow (SF); 100g (3½oz) red; 40g (1½oz) grey

firefighter's helmet cakes
Sugarpaste (rolled fondant) with CMC: 70g (2½oz) red; 60g (2¼oz) Melon Yellow (SF)

flame cakes
Sugarpaste (rolled fondant) with CMC: 50g (1¾oz) Melon Yellow (SF) and 20g (¾oz) red blended together

cops & robbers

bases
Sugarpaste (rolled fondant) with CMC: 250g (9oz) navy blue

police car cakes
Sugarpaste (rolled fondant) with CMC: 35g (1¼oz) white; 20g (¾oz) each yellow, blue and black

emergency cone cakes
Sugarpaste (rolled fondant) with CMC: 20g (¾oz) white; 50g (1¾oz) orange

handcuff cakes
Sugarpaste (rolled fondant) with CMC: 7g (¼oz) black and 30g (1oz) white blended together to make grey

super troopers

soldier cakes

Sugarpaste (rolled fondant) with CMC: 70g (2½oz) flesh-coloured (teddy bear brown and white blended together); 25g (1oz) dark bottle green; 7g (¼oz) teddy bear brown; 5g (⅛oz) each chocolate brown and light green; 7g (¼oz) white; 5g (⅛oz) black

medal cakes

Sugarpaste (rolled fondant) with CMC: 75g (2¾oz) chocolate brown; 50g (1¾oz) pale grey; 40g (1½oz) red, 30g (1oz) navy blue, 50g (1¾oz) white

tank track cakes

Sugarpaste (rolled fondant) with CMC: 75g (2¾oz) chocolate brown; 10g (¼oz) green

doctors & nurses

crosses & plasters

Sugarpaste (rolled fondant) with CMC: 60g (2¼oz) pale blue or white; 30g (1oz) each red and pinkish brown (teddy bear brown, white, red and orange blended together)

nurse cakes

Sugarpaste (rolled fondant) with CMC: 60g (2¼oz) flesh-coloured (peach); 35g (1¼oz) chocolate brown; 30g (1oz) white; 10g (¼oz) black; 7g (¼oz) red

doctor cakes

Sugarpaste (rolled fondant) with CMC: 60g (2¼oz) flesh-coloured (chocolate brown and teddy bear brown blended together); 50g (1¾oz) green; 7g (¼oz) white

pop idols

pop singer cakes
Sugarpaste (rolled fondant) with CMC: 60g (2¼oz) flesh-coloured (peach); 35g (1¼oz) yellow; 5g (⅛oz) purple; 20g (¾oz) black

musical note cakes
Sugarpaste (rolled fondant) with CMC: 60g (2¼oz) purple; 30g (1oz) yellow

microphone cakes
Sugarpaste (rolled fondant) with CMC: 60g (2¼oz) purple; 40g (1½oz) yellow; 20g (¾oz) each grey and black

fairytales & adventure

wicked pirates
Sugarpaste (rolled fondant) with CMC: 70g (2½oz) flesh-coloured (peach) for girl pirates; 70g (2½oz) flesh-coloured (teddy bear brown and white blended together), plus optional 10g (¼oz) chocolate brown for dark complexion for boy pirates; 75g (2¾oz) each red and pink; 70g (2½oz) white; 40g (1½oz) black

magical mermaids
Sugarpaste (rolled fondant) with CMC: 150g (5½oz) flesh-coloured (peach); 10g (¼oz) bright pink; 30g (1oz) white; 200g (7oz) chestnut brown

mini octopus cakes

Sugarpaste (rolled fondant) with CMC: 40g (1½oz) white; 20g (¾oz) pale blue; 120g (4½oz) yellow

fabulous fairies

Sugarpaste (rolled fondant) with CMC: 150g (5½oz) flesh-coloured (peach); 10g (¼oz) bright pink; 20g (¾oz) white; 150g (5½oz) pale yellow; 100g (3½oz) grey

mini wand cakes

Sugarpaste (rolled fondant) with CMC: 50g (1¾oz) lilac; 30g (1oz) each (1oz) yellow and pink

gallant knights

Sugarpaste (rolled fondant) with CMC: 140g (5oz) flesh-coloured of your choice (see Techniques: Using Sugarpaste); 150g (5½oz) grey; 20g (¾oz) red; 30g (1oz) black; 5g (⅛oz) white

mini sword cakes

Sugarpaste (rolled fondant) with CMC: 60g (2¼oz) black; 30g (1oz) grey; 20g (¾oz) red

suppliers

UK

Cakes 4 Fun
100 Lower Richmond Road,
Putney, London SW15 1LN
Tel: 020 8785 9039
www.cakes4funshop.co.uk
Bespoke cake creations, sugarcraft
shop and online shop stocking all
cake-making equipment used in this
book; sugarcraft school teaching
all forms of cake decoration.

Keylink Ltd
Green Lane, Ecclesfield,
Sheffield, S35 9WY
Tel: 01142 455400
www.keylink.org
Suppliers of Belgian Callebaut
chocolate callets and clear
presentation boxes.

Knightsbridge PME Ltd
Unit 23, Riverwalk Road
(off Jeffreys Road),
Enfield EN3 7QN
Tel: 020 3234 0049
www.cakedecoration.co.uk
Suppliers of plunger cutters,
modelling tools and cake
stands, and UK distributor of
Wilton Industries products.

RUCraft
Brunel House, Forde Close,
Newton Abbot, TQ12 4PU
Tel: 0844 880 5852
www.rucraft.co.uk
Sugarcraft and baking supplies.

Abbreviations
C4F = Cakes 4 Fun
DP = Diamond
Paste Moulds
FMM = FMM
Sugarcraft
PME = PME
Sugarcraft

SF = Sugarflair
WIL = Wilton

NB All sugarpaste
colours used in the
book are either
Regalice or M & B

USA

Global Sugar Art
625 Route 3, Unit 3,
Plattsburgh, NY 12901
Tel: + 1 518 561 3039
www.globalsugarart.com
Sugarcraft suppliers that also import
many UK products into the USA.

Kemper Enterprises Inc
13595 12th Street,
Chino, CA 91710
Tel: + 1 909 627 6191
www.kempertools.com
For mini plunger cutters and palette
knives – also available through all
good cake-decorating stores.

Wilton Industries
2240 West 75th Street,
Woodridge, IL 60517
Tel: + 1 800 794 5866
www.wilton.com
Cupcake cases (liners) and cake
stands.

about the author

Carolyn has always loved having fun with cakes, hence her company name Cakes 4 Fun! Everything she looks at is stored away as 'that could make a great cake one day', and this is just how she sees everything, from a handbag to a greetings card.

She started her cake-making business at home following redundancy and quickly grew it through her passion for fun novelty cakes and her eye for detail. The business has grown gradually and she has always welcomed new people to join it, enjoying sharing her techniques with fellow team members and learning from their varied experiences to help her continually keep the company fresh and exciting. From her Putney-based shop and online store, her cake business now encompasses novelty cakes, wedding and corporate cakes, cake-decorating supplies and a thriving tutoring enterprise teaching cake enthusiasts every style of cake decorating from cupcakes to 3D designer handbags.

Carolyn also wrote *Bake Me I'm Yours... Cake Pops*, so if you like this book, why not try your hand at creating some cake pops!

I would like to dedicate this book to: Jamie and Ella, who love cupcakes – particularly the icing!

acknowledgments

Many thanks to the whole David & Charles team for their professional approach, enthusiasm and support throughout the whole process – special thanks to James, Grace and Charly. Also thanks to Jo for her work on my text and to Sian, Nick and Joe for the amazing photography.

I would also like to say a special thanks to members of the Cakes 4 Fun team: my fellow cupcake enthusiast Samantha Harrison who joined me in the fun side of designing and creating the great cupcake ideas in this book. Also thanks to Simone Clarke, my operations manager, and her fantastic cake team, Celia, Jen, Adam and Pervin. Together they whizzed up the many recipes, road-tested them and helped with producing brilliant cakes for the final shoot. Thanks also to Sam's sons who made a super cake-tasting panel – Stevie, Adam and Danny always gave their honest opinion and munched their way through many a cupcake in the course of this book!

I would also like to thank Graham, my husband, without whose inspiration, support and time spent distracting the kids while I was working to deadlines this second book would never have existed.

index

A DAVID & CHARLES BOOK
© F&W Media International, Ltd 2012

David & Charles is an imprint of
F&W Media International, Ltd
Brunel House, Forde Close,
Newton Abbot, TQ12 4PU, UK

F&W Media International, Ltd is a
subsidiary of F+W Media, Inc
10151 Carver Road, Suite #200,
Blue Ash, OH 45242, USA

Text and Designs © Carolyn White 2012
Layout and Photography © F&W
Media International, Ltd 2012

First published in the UK and USA in 2012

Carolyn White has asserted her right to be identified
as author of this work in accordance with the
Copyright, Designs and Patents Act, 1988.

The author and publisher have made every effort
to ensure that all the instructions in the book are
accurate and safe, and therefore cannot accept
liability for any resulting injury, damage or loss
to persons or property, however it may arise.

Names of manufacturers and product ranges are
provided for the information of readers, with no
intention to infringe copyright or trademarks.

A catalogue record for this book is
available from the British Library.

ISBN-13: 978-1-4463-0242-2 hardback
ISBN-10: 1-4463-0242-3 hardback

Printed in China by RR Donnelley for:
F&W Media International, Ltd
Brunel House, Forde Close,
Newton Abbot, TQ12 4PU, UK

10 9 8 7 6 5 4 3 2 1

Acquisitions Editor: James Brooks
Assistant Editor: Grace Harvey
Project Editor: Jo Richardson
Art Editor: Charly Bailey
Photographer: Sian Irvine
Senior Production Controller: Kelly Smith

F+W Media publishes high-quality books
on a wide range of subjects.
For more great book ideas visit: www.rucraft.co.uk

loved this book?

For more inspiration, ideas and free downloadable projects visit

www.stitchcraftcreate.com

Bake Me I'm Yours...
Sweet Bitesize Bakes

Sarah Trivuncic
ISBN-13: 978-1-4463-0183-8

Bake miniature versions of your best-loved desserts, confections and sweet treats with these easy-to-follow recipes, including tasty fillings and toppings, from buttercream and chocolate ganache to marshmallow fluff, lemon curd and crème pâtissière.

Bake Me I'm Yours...
Cake Pops

Carolyn White
ISBN-13: 978-1-4463-0137-1

A delicious collection of fun cake pop treats for every occasion, with over 40 colourful projects, from cute animals and romantic wedding rings, to creepy Halloween creatures and festive Christmas characters!

Bake Me I'm Yours...
Whoopie Pies

Jill Collins & Natalie Saville
ISBN-13: 978-1-4463-0068-8

Discover over 70 designs that will make you shout 'whoopie!' These gorgeous (and tasty!) baked treats are organized into fun themed collections of coordinating whoopies for any celebration.

Bake Me I'm Yours...
Cupcake Celebration

Lindy Smith
ISBN-13: 978-0-7153-3770-7

Celebrate in style, with over 25 irresistible cupcake ideas from renowned sugarcrafter Lindy Smith. Add that special touch to every occasion with these amazing designs and tempting recipes, including sticky ginger, chocolate cherry and lemon polenta.

All details correct at time of printing.